Entire contents copyright © 2017 Lewis Trondheim and Brigitte Findakly. Translation copyright © 2017 Helge Dascher, with thanks to Peggy Burns, Dag Dascher, Tracy Hurren, John Kadlecek, and Laila Parsons. All rights reserved. No part of this book (except small portions for review purposes) may be reproduced in any form without written permission from Lewis Trondheim and Brigitte Findakly or Drawn & Quarterly. Production assistance by Nolwenn Guillemot. Originally published in French by L'Association.

drawnandquarterly.com | First edition: September 2017 | Printed in China | 10 9 8 7 6 5 4 3 2 1

Library and Archives Canada Cataloguing in Publication
Findakly, Brigitte [Coquelicots d'Irak. English]. Poppies of Iraq / Brigitte Findakly, Lewis Trondheim ; Helge Dascher, translator. Translation of: Coquelicots d'Irak. ISBN 978-1-77046-293-9 (hardcover) 1. Findakly, Brigitte—Childhood and youth—Comic books, strips, etc. 2. Women cartoonists—France—Biography— Comic books, strips, etc. 3. Women cartoonists—Iraq—Biography—Comic books, strips, etc. 4. Iraq— Social conditions--20th century—Comic books, strips, etc. 5. Iraq—History—1958-1979—Comic books, strips, etc. 6. Autobiographical comics. I. Trondheim, Lewis, author, illustrator II. Dascher, Helge, 1965–, translator III. Title. IV. Coquelicots d'Irak. English. PN6747.F554Z46 2017   741.5'944   C2017-901596-6

Published in the USA by Drawn & Quarterly, a client publisher of Farrar, Straus and Giroux. Orders: 888.330.8477. Published in Canada by Drawn & Quarterly, a client publisher of Raincoast Books. Orders: 800.663.5714. Published in the United Kingdom by Drawn & Quarterly, a client publisher of Publishers Group UK. Orders: info@pguk.co.uk.

Canada Drawn & Quarterly acknowledges the support of the Government of Canada and the Canada Council for the Arts for our publishing program, and the National Translation Program for Book Publishing, an initiative of the Roadmap for Canada's Official Languages 2013–2018: Education, Immigration, Communities, for our translation activities.

Drawn & Quarterly reconnaît l'aide financière du gouvernement du Québec par l'entremise de la Société de développement des entreprises culturelles (SODEC) pour nos activités d'édition. Gouvernement du Québec—Programme de crédit d'impôt pour l'édition de livres—Gestion SODEC.

Cet ouvrage a bénéficié du soutien des Programmes d'aide à la publication de l'Institut français.

BRIGITTE FINDAKLY - LEWIS TRONDHEIM

POPPIES of IRAQ

Cowritten by
Brigitte Findakly & Lewis Trondheim

Drawn by
Lewis Trondheim

Colored by
Brigitte Findakly

Translated by
Helge Dascher

DRAWN & QUARTERLY

Parts of this book were previously published in the *La Matinale* app
and on the website LeMonde.fr.

The authors would like to thank Frédéric Potet for having set the story in motion,
David B. for his thoughtful feedback, and François Corteggiani for the
initial loan of the pots of paint.

Their warmest thanks go also to Jacqueline, Matti, and Dominique Findakly,
without whom none of this would have been possible.

Every Friday we would go for a picnic outside Mosul.

And often, we'd wind up at the archaeological site of Nimrud.

I'd play ball and climb on anything I could.

Hold still, I'm going to take a photo.

Come on!

If my father had known those winged lions would be destroyed one day, I'm sure he would have framed the shot differently.

On March 7, 2015, the site of
Hatra was leveled with dynamite
and bulldozers.

Because it's 130 km
from Mosul, we picnicked
there less often.

It was the perfect spot
for climbing around on ancient stones.

And for picking poppies.

They'll wilt
right away,
honey.

But taking stones
was strictly forbidden.

Cars were searched on
their way out to preserve
the site forever.

In 1947, my father, Matti, left Iraq to study dentistry in France.

One of his brothers, Jacques, had studied architecture there.

Another brother, Behnam, earned his engineering degree in India.

And a last brother, Salem, studied medicine in Syria.

Thirty years later, Iraqi universities offered training in all fields, and their degrees were recognized worldwide.

Parents didn't have to send their children abroad anymore.

But then my father wouldn't have met my mother on a platform at the St. Lazare station.

My parents were married in Paris in 1950. My father returned to Iraq right after, just long enough to let the family know.

But his mother had found him a fiancée in Baghdad.

For six months, he didn't dare say anything.

On the way back from a visit to the fiancée's family, he finally confessed to his mother that he'd already gotten married in France.

His mother never did give him the tailored suit she'd ordered for his wedding.

And my mother didn't exactly get a warm reception when she finally arrived.

But because she was from a country that had been through five years of war, people were polite enough to accept her.

Skinny, isn't she?

They have nothing to eat there...

To this day, some 95 percent of marriages in Iraq are arranged.

Since the 1980s though, with the heightened surveillance under Saddam Hussein, people have grown distrustful of each other and many marriages are between first cousins.

Since my father was Orthodox Christian, I was baptized by an Orthodox priest.

And since my mother was Catholic, I was baptized a second time by a Catholic priest.

I went to a public elementary school, Abu Tammam...

Christians were excused from Quran lessons.

I found myself in the playground while the others stayed in class.

Feeling left out and rejected, I cried bitterly. And I told the whole story when I got home.

My father went to see the principal and, after that, I sat in on all Quran lessons.

We memorized verses from the Quran, without much explanation.

When I got to sixth grade, my parents enrolled me in Oum Elmaouna, a school run by Syriac Catholic nuns, so I could receive my first communion.

I memorized prayers in Aramean that I didn't understand either.

None of which made me a believer.

I got a watch.

And I'm dressed like a bride.

Especially since I switched to another public school the year after my communion.

It's funny, I don't remember the name of that school...

But my friend Nadwa, who emigrated to San Diego five months ago, would probably know.

Huh?

Oh, wow...

It's Nadwa.

That still doesn't make me a believer.

It's just a coincidence.

Nadwa was the daughter of our neighbors in Mosul.

A door led from one garden to the other... We spent a lot of time together.

And since they were Muslim, I did my Quran homework with her mother.

The last time I saw Nadwa was in 1989, before the first Gulf War.

In June 2014, she and her husband rented an apartment in Erbil, in Iraqi Kurdistan, for a two-week vacation.

They left without a worry, packing only for their trip.

The next day, Daesh* invaded Mosul.

Nadwa and her husband would never see their city again.

After their two weeks in Erbil, they couldn't afford to extend their stay.

Costs had sky-rocketed with the influx of refugees.

There's no loss without gain...

*Arabic term for the group also known as ISIS or ISIL.

Once a week during the three months of summer, all the neighborhood kids would be outside having the time of their lives.

Except my brother and me...

Our parents kept us indoors and shut all the windows when the city came spraying DDT to control the mosquitoes.

My mother subscribed to a women's magazine that came from France every month.

There were always holes in the second-to-last page, where the "Hit Parade" photos were.

She said they were the Enrico Macias records.

It was years before I asked my mother why.

Customs officials had to cut out his photos because he was Jewish.

In Iraq

So?

Completely.

So?
Completely.

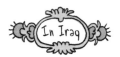

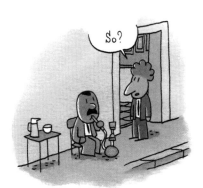

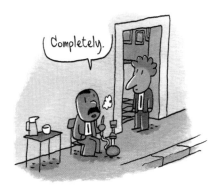

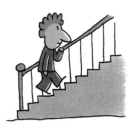

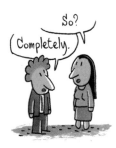

In Iraq, before a wedding, the
future husband is asked if he wants
his fiancée's pubic hair completely
removed or left as is.

A while back, my brother managed to trace our family tree back to the year 300.

We're descendents of the Banu Taghlib, a Christian Arab tribe that came from the Arabian Peninsula between 300 and 600 to settle in Tikrit, the center of Syriac Christianity.

Later, in the 1200s, the Mongol invasions pushed us north to Mosul, where the family became entirely sedentary.

Seven generations ago, in the days of the Ottoman Empire, my forefather's name was not Findakly, but Alnakkar.

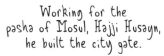

Alnakkar means "sculptor."

And fittingly, he was a mason and a stonecutter.

Working for the pasha of Mosul, Hajji Husayn, he built the city gate.

In 1743, the Persians tried to invade Mosul. They held it under siege for forty days before finally leaving.

Because the gate had withstood the Persian assault, the pasha decided to grant my forefather Simaan Alnakkar the name Findakly, which means a kind of precious gold.

Generations later, my father's father was a sculptor too.

And although he was Christian, he helped to restore the Mosque of Nabi Sheet, built in the eleventh century.

Like many Mosulite mosques containing the tombs of scholars, philosophers, or prophets, it was recently destroyed by the Wahhabi Islamists of Daesh.

For a while they were also planning to destroy Muhammad's tomb in Medina, but then for whatever reason, they reconsidered.

We always spoke French at home and Arabic outside.

My mother ended up learning a bit of Arabic and got by pretty well, despite her accent.

My father was a dentist in the army but he also had a private dental clinic in town.

The few times he went to Baghdad, he'd call my mother and they would speak in French.

Every time, a censor assigned to monitor the private conversations of military personnel would cut in and chastise them.

*Speak in Arabic or hang up!

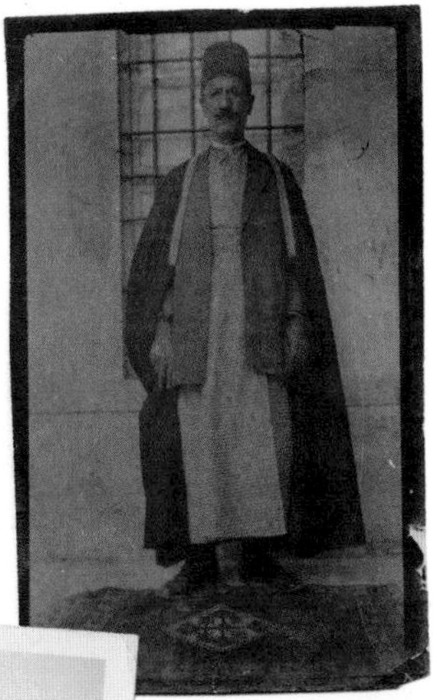

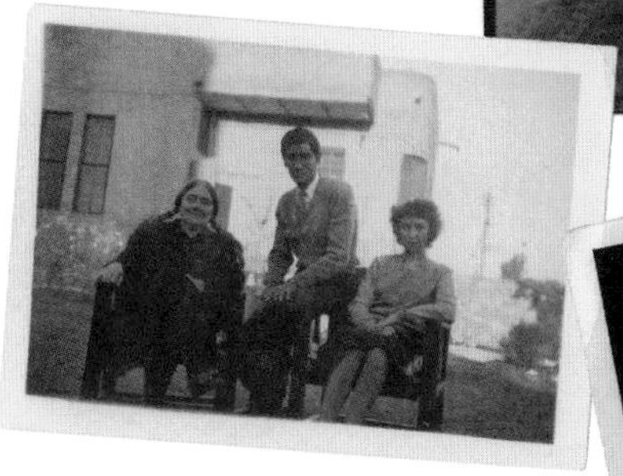

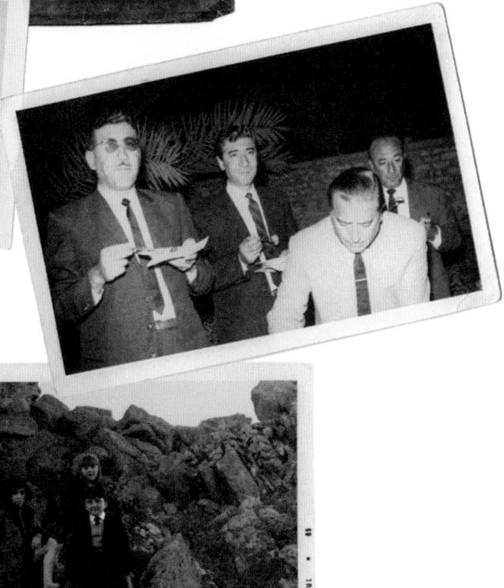

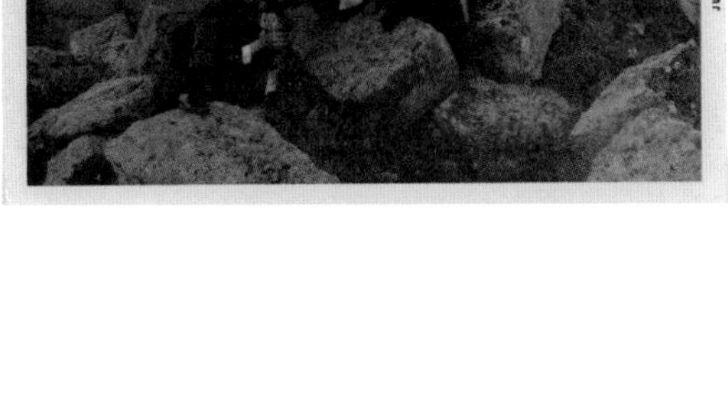

In July 1958, the government was overthrown in a coup. King Faysal II and his family and servants were executed.

Abd al-Karim Qasim was named commander of the armed forces, defence minister, and prime minister.

In the turbulent months that followed, soldiers entered homes and stole anything of value.

My father was called up for active duty.

And, one evening when he was away, soldiers rang at our house.

What do you want?

Open up!

Wait! I'll call my husband, he's in the army.

Okay, fine. Forget it.

We're going...

A few months later, my mother was pregnant with me. My father was afraid to leave her alone.

One day, he brought her a gun so she could protect herself at home.

My mother was very, very afraid of that gun.

As soon as my father left again, she buried it in the garden.

It's probably still there...

In 1963, there was a new coup, this time led by the Baath Party.

And General Qasim was executed.

Since he had lined up with the Soviet Bloc, communists in Iraq were now harshly suppressed, including those affiliated with the Baath party.

My mother was indirectly affected...

...because everything red was strictly banned in the streets and in public places.

She had to put her pretty red purse away in the closet.

In Iraq

In Iraq, it is considered good manners to refuse second helpings.

The hostess must insist repeatedly, and only then is it polite to accept.

My mother made wonderful French desserts that everybody loved.

When she'd offer seconds, the guests would politely refuse, waiting for her to insist.

Which she never did.

It was a custom my mother never got used to... Instead, it was the guests who finally changed their ways when they came to visit.

In 1958, Generals Arif and Qasim overthrew the monarchy.

Arif was for Iraqi entry into the United Arab Republic, and Qasim, a nationalist, was against it. Arif was arrested and sentenced to death, then pardoned and exiled.

In 1963, General Arif returned and mounted a coup against Qasim with the support of the Baathists.

A year later, he decided to have the Baathists executed too.

In Mosul, Baathist militiamen, who weren't popular to begin with (notorious, among other things, for extortion, torture, and burying prisoners alive), were publicly hanged.

My brother, who was nine years old, was taken by bus with his class to see the hanged men.

In 1966, General Arif died in a helicopter accident.

On the day of his funeral, symbolic coffins were carried through Iraq's major cities.

Teachers had to line their students up along the route and, according to my brother, were required to display their grief by crying.

Two years later, General Arif's brother, who had succeeded him, came to Mosul.

The only school outing I remember is when we went to wait for him near the airport, saluting proudly as he passed by.

In 1968, he wanted to introduce democracy and a multi-party system. Just before the enactment of this law, Baathists overthrew him.

When you crossed the al-Jadid bridge into our neighborhood, our house was the first one you saw.

The Baathists, who were in power at the time, had painted the slogan "Long Live the Baath Party" on our wall so it was clearly visible to those arriving.

Our backyard neighbor, with whom we got along well, was pro-Nasser. One day, his kids, who were about fifteen, decided to cross out the propaganda.

Baathists came to our door, but seeing that my mother was French and my father in the army, they quickly understood that we weren't responsible.

So they rang at the neighbor's, whom they vaguely suspected of being a Nasserist. The two teens immediately came to hide in our basement.

They stayed for two days before daring to go back home.

The authorities quickly had the wall repainted in its original color to avoid having another slogan crossed out.

From 1963 on, we spent every summer in France.

In Paris, we always stayed at the same hotel, on Rue de l'Abbé-de-l'Épée.

We ended up becoming friends with the owners.

In the summer of 1969, they were relieved to see us arrive.

They had heard on the news that many people had been hanged in Iraq.

I didn't know anything about it.

As it turned out, the government had executed the last Jewish merchants still living in Iraq... They'd been falsely accused of being spies.

In 1966, my mother ordered a dictionary.

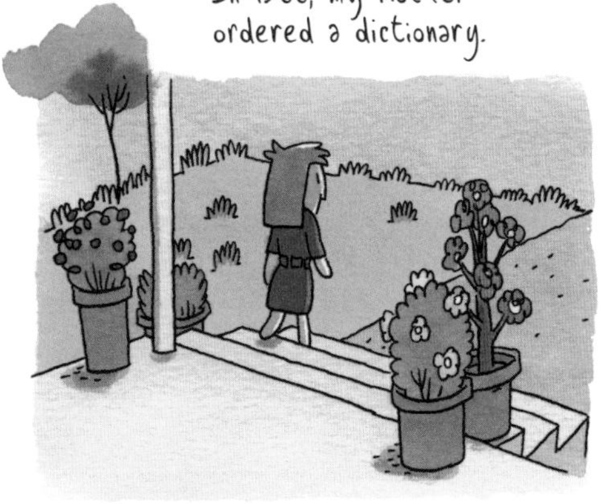

When we got it, we immediately looked up the entry for Iraq.

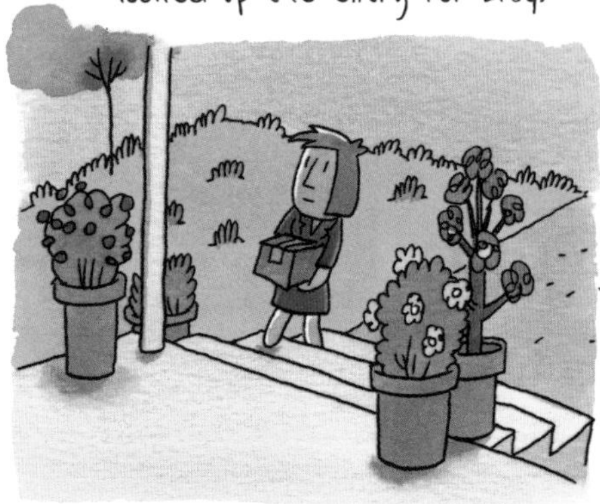

But the page was torn out.

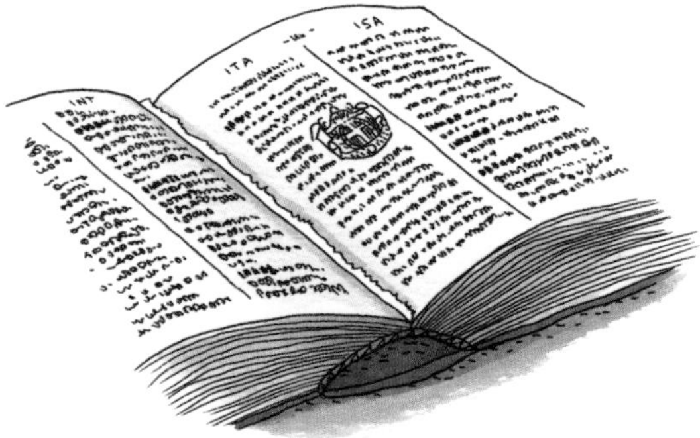
INT
ITA
ISA

It hadn't been censored to hide information about Iraq...

...but to remove the entry about Israel included on the same page.

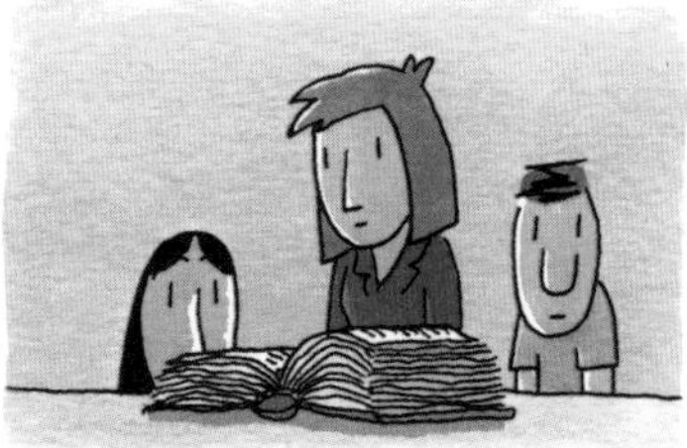

The first time I heard the word Israel was in 1973, when we moved to France.

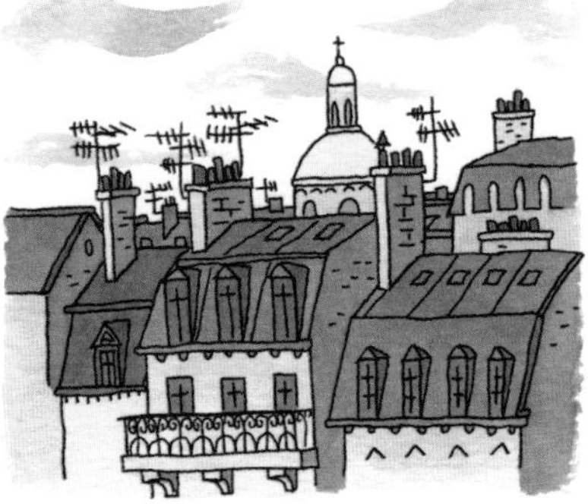

Before that, I'd heard about "the occupied land" in the news, but that was all.

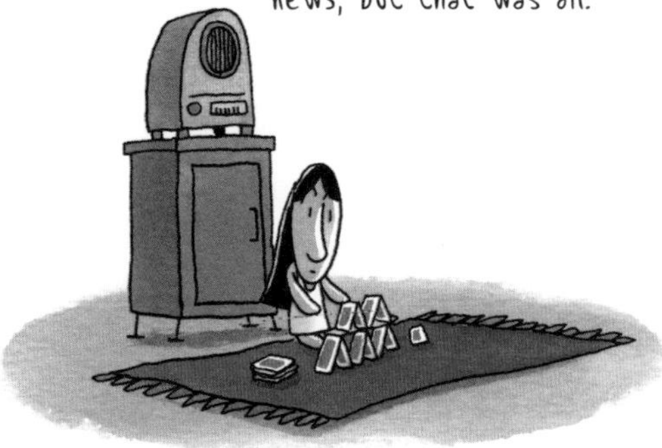

Every morning in elementary school, we lined up by class in the schoolyard for the raising of the flag.

We sang the national anthem.

My homeland, my homeland, Glory and beauty and splendor are in your hills...

Then the teachers checked to see if our nails were clean.

We would hold out our hands, palms down, clutching a handkerchief.

You could only use it to blow your nose, but you had to have one.

Uniforms were mandatory to create a sense of social equality among the students.

But everyone could tell who the poor kids were. Their uniforms were shabby hand-me-downs, and their shirts were rarely ironed.

Every week, the best groomed boy and girl were assigned to be class representatives. None of the poor kids were ever chosen.

The poor students sat at the back of the classroom without being told, and every week, when two volunteers were needed to do the cleaning, they were the only ones to put up their hands.

I volunteered for cleaning duty once...All the students gave me a strange look, like I was a bit dimwitted.

I never understood why the poor kids sat at the back of the class, or why they volunteered for the thankless tasks.

Through all the turbulence and the coups of the 1960s, I only felt in danger once.

I was with my brother and mother in a café. We had just been served.

The staff suddenly seemed agitated. A waiter came to tell us that a demonstration was approaching and that everybody had to leave because they were closing immediately.

We found ourselves in the street. All the cafés were closing... And then we heard the roar of a wave of protestors coming toward us. We followed the other people seeking safety in a subway station.

It was June 1968, on Boulevard St. Michel in the Latin Quarter, during the last aftershocks of May '68.

I told myself France was dangerous.

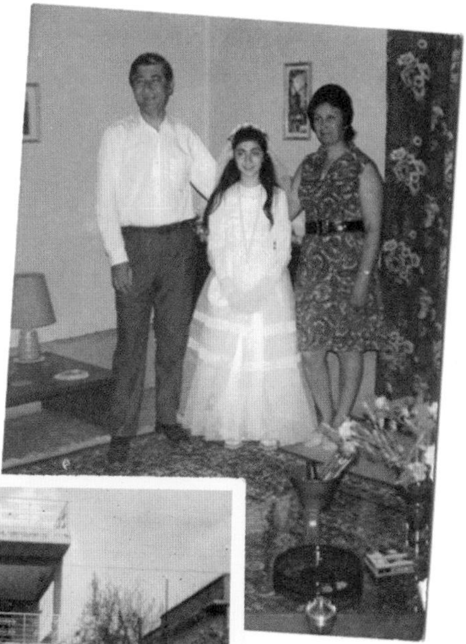

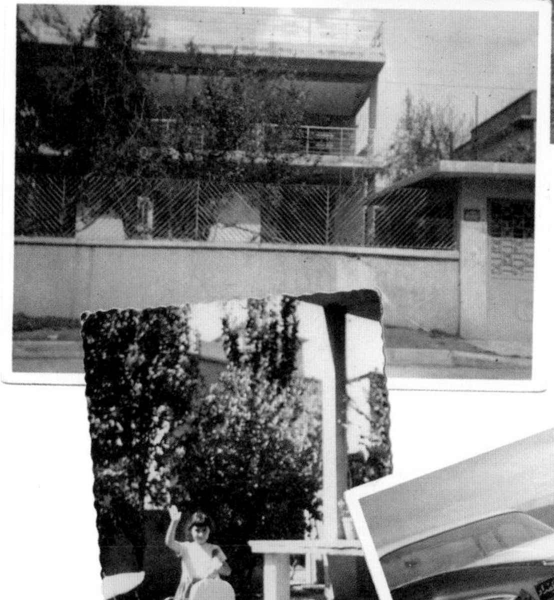

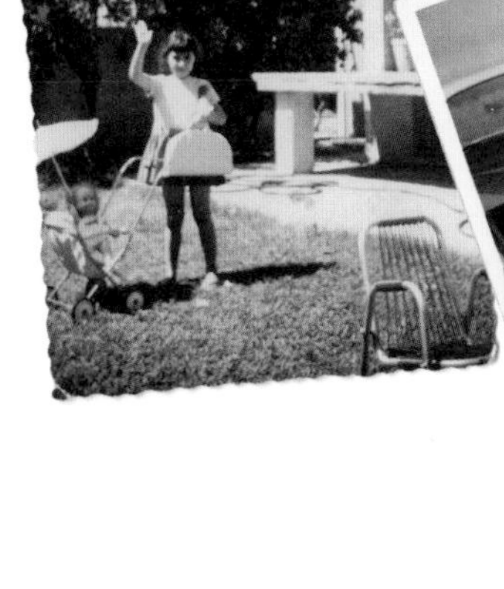

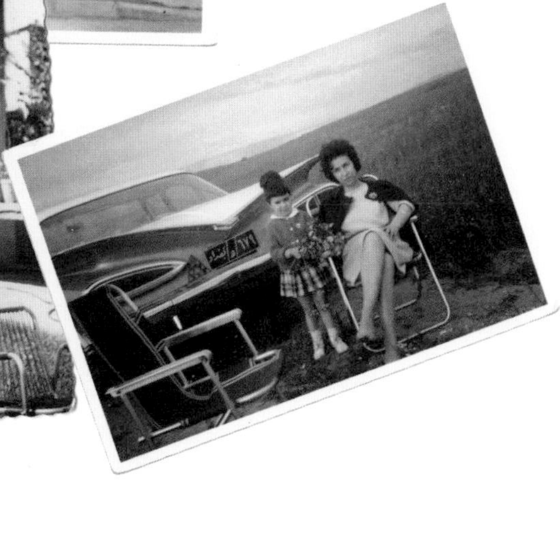

My mother and father live right across the street from me. They're eighty-nine and ninety-one years old...

My mother calls to tell me that her one remaining brother, Lucien, just passed away...

One of Lucien's sons, my cousin, found out about my mother's existence seven years ago and got in touch with her.

She was the youngest of six children, and she was six years younger than Lucien. When she was born, some of her brothers and sisters were already married.

My mother was thirteen when her mother died. Her father married the maid and my mother was sent to board with nuns. After that, her family cut off all contact with her.

Which probably explains why my mother didn't think twice about leaving France to live so far way.

And now here I am, fifty-five years old and I've only ever been to one funeral, and I'm trying to write a letter of condolence to a cousin I've only met twice.

In Iraq

In Iraq, it's the men who do the groceries.

When they moved to Mosul, my parents needed a doctor for my brother.

They discovered the doctor they'd been referred to spoke French. As it turned out, his wife, Madeleine, was from France.

My parents saw them often. Madeleine became my godmother. And she tried to encourage us to be more devout.

Before your piano lesson, we'll pray.

My mother quickly distanced herself from the constant proselytizing. But the two couples kept up a cordial friendship.

Then came the years of spying and paranoia.

The army asked my father to read all incoming and outgoing mail written in French...But my father didn't want to, and he delegated the task to my mother.

So she found herself reading the letters Madeleine sent to her family, saying how much she liked Dr. Findakly and disliked his wife.

After the fall of the monarchy in 1958, Israel began broadcasting a radio show in Arabic every Friday at 8:00 p.m. It ran for more than twenty years.

The program was called *The Son of Mesopotamia*. It was the only source of uncensored news about the government and what was happening in Iraq.

Those who listened to it ran the risk of a stiff prison sentence... But the show was a favorite and everybody tuned in on Fridays...

...even government officials, who couldn't figure out where the leaks were coming from.

In 1970, I got a little radio for Christmas. But I never listened to *The Son of Mesopotamia*.

In my room, I was tuned to the *Voice of America* so I could hear the English-language pop songs of the day.

In Iraq, friends, family, neighbors, and acquaintances would visit each other unannounced.

It annoyed my father, who could never say no but would quietly prompt my mother to cut things short.

Our maid, unlike those in other families, was allowed to sit in a chair behind us to watch TV.

But when my father came home tired, he'd ask my mother to send her away.

My mother wasn't always considered especially friendly.

But everybody loved my father.

In the early '70s, the government supplied farmers with wheat coated in red pesticide.

It specified that these were high quality, insect-resistant seeds. And that they were to be used only for planting.

Many farmers ignored the warning. They fed the grain to their livestock and poultry, which then died in massive numbers.

Some farmers ate the grain themselves, mistaking the coating for tomato sauce. Many fell ill and some even became blind.

Those who were spared realized the grain was no good and dumped the rest into the river, contaminating the fish.

Every kind of meat was prohibited in Mosul for almost two months. Which is when we discovered corned beef...

The national pastime in Iraq was gossip, and it still is.

When people got together, all they ever talked about was other people.

Movie theaters showed nothing anymore except Egyptian and Indian films full of singing and crying. You couldn't have much of a conversation about those.

The same went for literature, with very few Arabic books available and even fewer English-language imports.

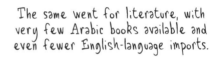

And political talk was becoming increasingly dangerous...

So people took real pleasure in talking about their acquaintances, and of course, they hated to be talked about.

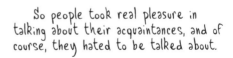

In conversation, people would avoid saying anything deep or intimate out of fear it might get repeated or even distorted.

Image and appearance mattered a lot, for individuals and even whole families.

For instance, a cousin who was an engineer fell in love with a woman from a wealthier background...

My family decided against asking the parents for her hand to avoid the potential shame of refusal...

So he married a first cousin instead.

My mother never gossiped or spread rumors during these conversations...

...and so people would come see her in private, to confide in her and discuss more personal matters.

One neighbor, who had lost all confidence in the banks, even entrusted her money to my mother.

The receptionist at my father's dental clinic had a younger sister, Anissa, who was fourteen.

Since my parents needed help around the house, they had her come from her village...
She was housed, fed, paid, and dressed.

Not wanting store-bought clothes, she chose her own fabrics and had them sewn up by the seamstress in her village.

She was five years older than me when she moved in with us. I taught her some reading, but we preferred playing together.

I'd often help her with the dishes so we could get around to playing faster.

Sometimes, I'd tell her to hide the dirty dishes under the sink so we could go have fun.

But we got caught one day and never did it again.

After Anissa turned seventeen, my mother noticed strange goings-on upstairs where her room was.

When my mother questioned her about it, Anissa got angry and walked out.

When she didn't come back, my mother got worried and asked friends in the street about her. She found out that Anissa had been flirting with a young neighbor from her window.

Anissa's brother was called. He went to the neighbor's, where she was hiding out, and took her back to the village.

We also had a man who came to clean. But then my mother made a comment one day and he was gone.

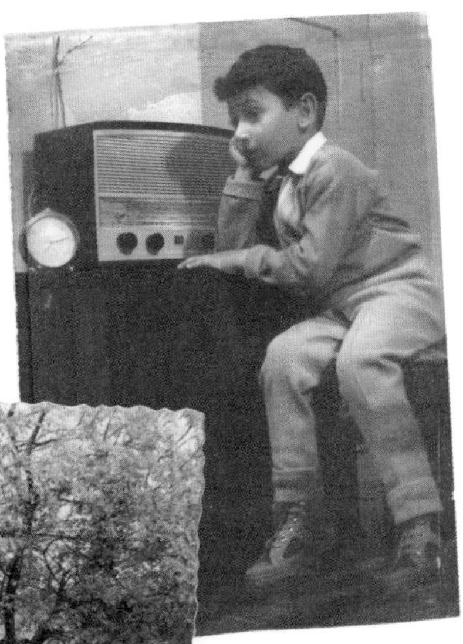

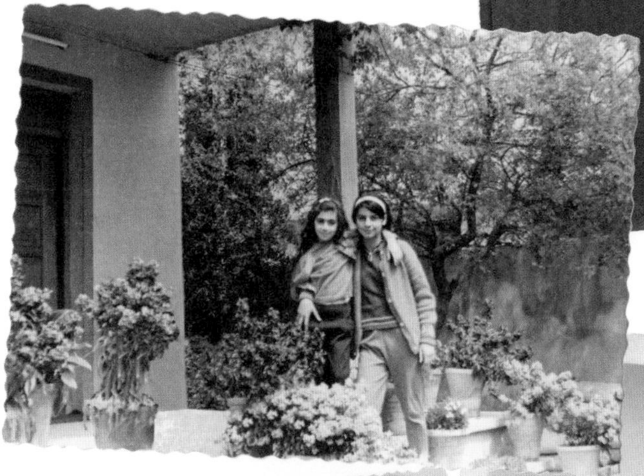

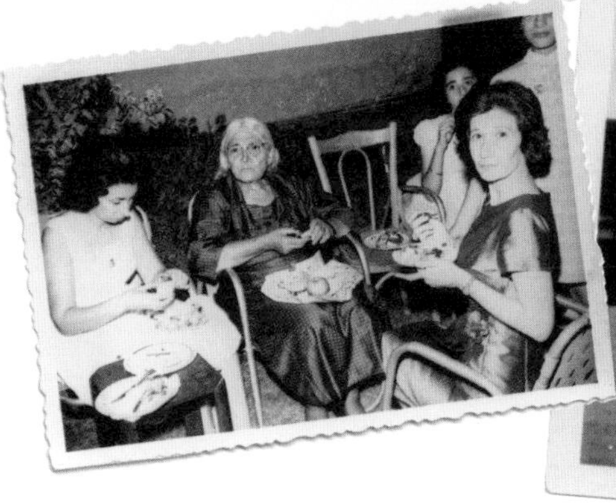

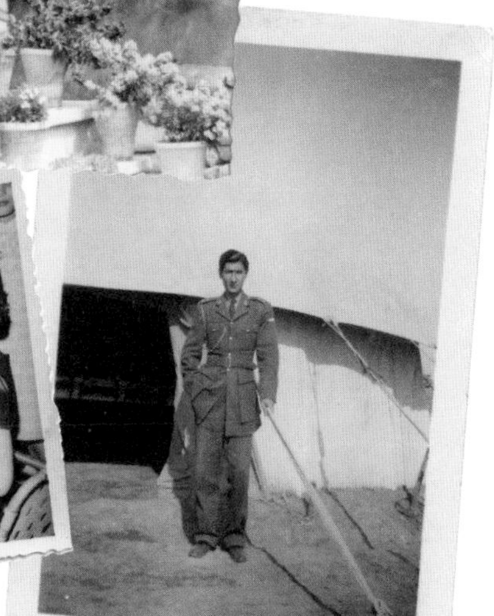

My cousin Ikram and her husband lived in Baghdad until 2007. But since they were relatively well-off, they worried about their three sons being kidnapped for ransom, a frequent occurrence in their part of town.

Their house had a guard and their children were driven to and from school by a chauffeur...

The rest of the time, the children weren't allowed out.

One day, one of the sons got angry and said he would rather risk death than be stuck in that prison.
So Ikram and her husband decided that they all had to leave Iraq.

They spent three years in Homs, Syria, and just before the civil war broke out, they got their visas to settle in Vancouver.

It's November 13, 2015, and Ikram calls to check if I'm all right, after today's terror attacks in Paris.

She asks me to stay inside. I promise, just to reassure her. Even though I live 750 km outside of Paris, in a quiet neighborhood.

A cousin who has lived in New Zealand for fifteen years calls me after the Paris attacks.

It's because of the Muslims.

According to an expert here in New Zealand, the Quran says to kill all non-Muslims.

But that's ridiculous.

It's not even about religion.

They're barbarians who are just using religion as a pretext to gain power.

No, no... You were too young to remember how they were.

They might seem friendly, but you can't trust them.

They're rotten to the core... They can't accept any religion other than their own.

I don't want to get angry at her.

It's no use.

And so little still connects me to Iraq.

I wonder what she meant when she said I was too young to remember.

I call my brother.

He tells me that after the coup in 1958 when General Qasim seized power, General Shawwaf was responsible for the Mosul region.

In 1959, Shawwaf staged a revolt against General Qasim, accusing him of having handed Iraq over to Communists.

And so Qasim sent planes to bomb Shawwaf's headquarters at the Mosul airport, next to the military hospital where my father worked.

After the bombing, Shawwaf sought refuge inside the hospital, but was followed by soldiers loyal to Qasim.

He was caught and killed, kicked to death in the room next to where my father was.

I cross the street to see my mother.

She tells me that Mosul residents, for fear of being labeled as supporters of the uprising and to avoid retaliation, displayed portraits of Qasim on their doors.

My mother did the same, of course.

After that incident, in 1960, a group of Christians in Mosul passed themselves off as pro-Qasim Communists.

Over several weeks, they ransacked and burned down the homes of the Muslim elite.

And I saw the owners... They tied them to cars and dragged them through the streets.

Why did they do that?

Who knows...

Some say it was vengeance. After the fall of the monarchy in 1958, the elite were spared, even though they'd supported the king.

Or maybe it was because they owned many surrounding villages that were home to very poor Christians.

The inequality triggered it all.

Or else, it was a personal settling of accounts...

Do you remember the Al-Mufti family?

In 1962, we moved into the house right next door to theirs.

Their new house, I mean... The other one had been pillaged and destroyed.

But they were able to get out with their lives.

So when we moved in next door, they were very leery.

Although Iraqis traditionally bring food to new neighbors, they didn't come and wouldn't speak to us.

Just because we were Christian.

Then, after a while, their daughter Nadwa became your best friend, we opened the door between our gardens, and we became very, very close.

In fact, it was Nadwa's mother who had me safeguard her money.

They were amazed that we could be so friendly and honest as Christians.

Later, after Qasim's ousting in 1963, Arif came to power, backed by a branch of the Muslim Brotherhood.

In 1964, Muslim fanatics wanted to get even for what had happened four years earlier.

Many Christians were assassinated, but mostly the ones responsible for what happened in 1960.

During this period, like many Christians who felt unsafe, my father would come home at 5:00 p.m. to avoid being out at night.

One evening, his boss called him in. My father hesitated to go, fearing for his life.

But finally his boss told him he didn't need to leave work at 5:00 p.m. The boss said he knew my father and the kind of man he was, and that nothing would happen to him, because my father treated everybody and spoke to all, without prejudice.

Still, a rift had opened between Christians and Muslims in Iraq.

Hello, this is Nadwa...

I heard about the attacks in Paris. Are you okay?

But it mostly affected those who were very devout and kept to their own.

In Iraq

Starting in 1969, a message came up on the screen before the start of every movie.

حفاظا على سلامة الوطن نحذر المواطنين
من الجواسيس واعداء الشعب والمندسين.
ارصدوا تحركات هؤلاء المشبوهين
واتصلوا بنا على الهاتف التالي *

*For the security of the nation, we warn citizens to beware of spies, enemies of the people, and intruders colluding with foreign powers. To report suspects, call the following number...

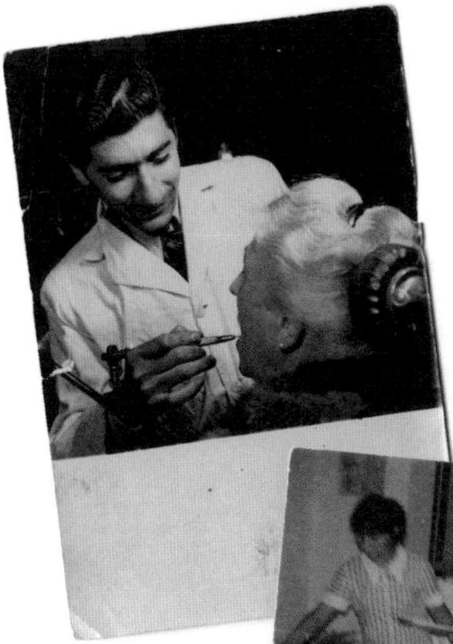
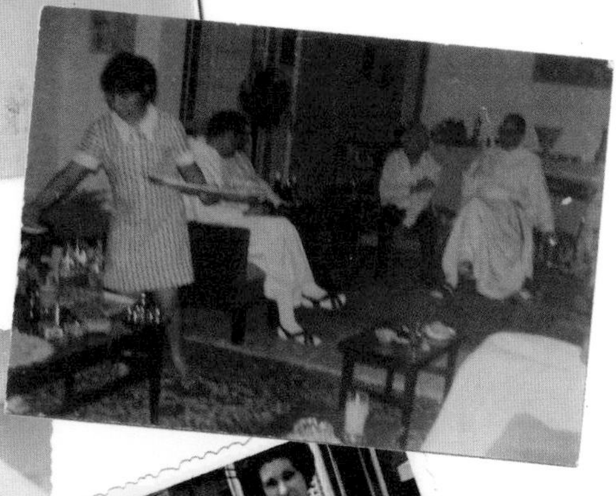
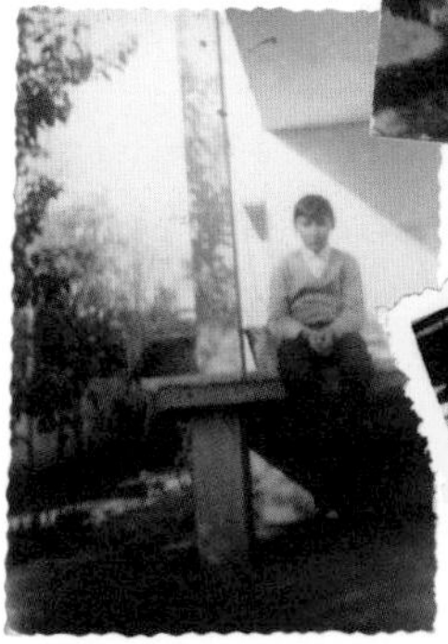
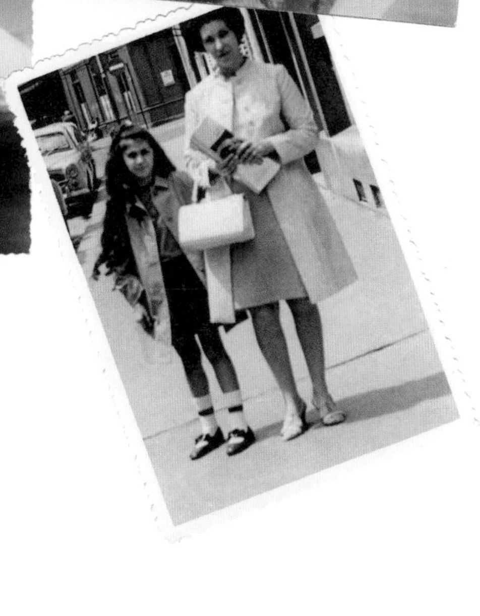

The poorest would go from door to door to ask for food.

We'd give them the leftover rice in one plastic bag and any other remainders in a second.

But one time when we went to the door with our mother, we saw a Palestinian refugee who was begging.

She opened her abaya and we saw that she was totally naked underneath. It was her way of showing that she had nothing.

Over the following years, it became common knowledge that many Palestinian women were begging for money in this way.

And our mother didn't want us answering the door with her anymore.

Since there was no cafeteria at school, my mother made us sandwiches for lunch.

My brother told her he didn't want any more of her egg and corned beef sandwiches. Instead, he wanted the tomato and hamba (spiced mango) sandwiches sold outside the school.

Dubious of the hygiene of the street vendors and wanting to be sure that my brother was eating well, my mother forced her homemade sandwiches on him.

So, before leaving for school, my brother would add the day's sandwich to the pile in his bedroom closet.

Of course, one day my mother opened the closet and dozens of moldy sandwiches tumbled out. My brother got an earful, and my mother continued making the same lunches for him.

After that, my brother switched to tossing my mother's sandwiches into an empty lot on the way to school.

I was six years younger than my brother, and at my school, we couldn't go out into the street to buy food at lunch.

At school, they sold potato-onion sandwiches. But I could never have any because my mother always made my lunches.

No!

A potato sandwich! That's just nonsense...

One time, I ended up trading mine for the potato sandwich a friend had bought.

It was really good!

Then, after 1971, foods like butter, eggs, and some fruits and vegetables became scarce. Everything was being exported to Kuwait.

Luckily, since we were good customers, our butcher put aside for us some of the butter and eggs he rounded up in neighboring villages.

During that time, the sandwiches at school were made with a new and much yellower product: margarine! It looked delicious to me...

I'd like margarine instead.

In Iraq

In Iraq, if a couple was sterile, a brother or sister would often end up giving them one of their babies at birth.

In 1970, the regime introduced "people's work campaigns," first in Baghdad, and then across the country, Mosul included.

My brother had just turned sixteen and would soon be subject to the new measure, which required high school and university students to spend their summers doing farm or construction work in rural areas and villages.

There were songs glorifying the Baath Party to rally the students.

They didn't really mind going, since the camps were mixed and thus promised some fun as well.

The most enthusiastic were encouraged to join the party and then the People's Army.

This army became the Baath Party Militia, intended as a counterforce to the official army.

Later, those who had a party card got public sector jobs more easily.

My father was wary and didn't want my brother going to the camps. And so in the summer of 1970, we went to France as usual for our vacation, leaving before the reform reached Mosul.

My brother wasn't crazy about the idea of finding himself alone in France for the school year. But I was jealous of him.

Old MacDonald had a farm e-i-e-i-oh!!!!

And, up until 1980, young people who had not gone to the camps were not allowed to leave Iraq.

My mother arranged for my brother to stay at a children's home in the Antibes in September and got him enrolled in a private school.

They're going to the beach for the day. Want to join them?

No.

Can I go?

I imagined that life in France would be a never-ending vacation.

e-i-e-i-o!

In 1971, a new law required all civil servants, the military included, who were married abroad to either get a divorce or resign.

My father decided to take early retirement from his work as an army dentist and started practicing full-time at his private clinic in town.

He treated everybody...And when patients were broke, he didn't charge them.

Same rate for friends and acquaintances. He didn't like to turn anybody away...

And since there was no system for reporting income, a tax official would spend a day in the waiting room, count <u>every</u> <u>patient</u>, then estimate a total for the year.

Being the generous pushover that he was, my father never got rich.

One morning, probably on a Friday because I had no school that day, my mother woke me up very early.

I put on my bathrobe and my mother had me go out into the garden.

There was a centimeter of snow on everything... I had never seen snow before.

I kind of pushed some snow together with my hands, just to see.

I didn't try to make a snowman. At the time, I didn't even know what a snowman was.

Less than two hours later, it was all gone, and it never snowed again.

In 1972, President Ahmed Hassan al-Bakr and his Vice President, Saddam Hussein, decided to nationalize Iraqi oil.

Other oil-producing nations in the Gulf, including Saudi Arabia, followed suit, setting off the 1973 oil crisis.

In school, our history and geography teacher asked us to draw a picture about it, even though we'd never had a drawing class.

I applied myself and drew an oil rig with people in front carrying a banner that said: "Arab oil for Arabs."

Being right in line with party ideology, my drawing got a lot of praise, and I was very proud that it was the only one put up in the hallway.

If my family had stayed in Iraq, I might have become a famous propaganda artist for Saddam Hussein's regime.

Doctors would treat patients
by giving them injections.

I never knew what
was being injected.

Some doctors would line their
patients up in a row and inject one
after the other, all with the
same needle, of course.

One doctor became a billionaire
and owned many buildings and
properties in Mosul.

When a doctor would only
prescribe medication, patients
would ask why they weren't
getting shots.

And they wouldn't go back,
assuming he was incompetent.

My mother calls to say that my father wants to speak with me.

After his stroke fifteen years ago, he began suffering a slow mental decline. And over the past two years, he has been deteriorating more quickly.

He had frequent dizzy spells that resulted in falls, some more serious than others.

When he would read, he'd have a harder time making sense of things, and now that his sight has declined, he can't read at all anymore.

For a while, I gave him sketch-books and he spent hours every day drawing compulsively.

If I didn't have this, I'd go crazy...

And there was a stretch when he would hear sounds, or a kind of music, and sometimes even a woman singing.

His sight continued to decline. He went from a walker to a wheelchair, and from the wheelchair to a hospital bed and total loss of autonomy.

He's having more and more trouble recognizing people. Sometimes he's fully aware of his state.

I've had enough.

I don't want to go on like this.

I'm going to kill myself.

I want you to be there so you can say I did it.

I don't want the police accusing your mother.

I spoke with him for a long time, repeating things, telling him we love him and that it's not up to us to decide these things.

I left feeling very sad, but not too worried. I knew he had no way of committing suicide.

In 1972, my father decided
to leave Iraq.

Every summer, he'd request
permission to join us on holiday,
but in ten years he was only
authorized to go three times.

Plus a dentist who had less
work and was envious of my
father spread rumors about him,
which made my father miserable.

Having been in the military, he
couldn't simply go as he wished since
he might be mobilized anytime.

And in the two years that my
brother had been living alone in
France, he hadn't been allowed
out of the country at all.

There were also the tax officials
who assessed my father based on all
his patients even though everybody
knew he treated many for free, and
so his taxes kept going up.

And to top it off, basic supplies were getting harder to come by, making everyday life more difficult.

It all added up to my father's decision to leave. My mother wasn't convinced.

The way my father saw it, we'd return once things improved.

But that was underestimating all the adversity ahead...

...with Saddam Hussein becoming president in 1979, the Iran-Iraq war from 1980 to '89, the Gulf War in 1990, the economic sanctions that followed, the second Gulf War in 2003, and now Daesh.

My mother had integrated well in Iraq, except for a few local customs she could never adapt to. Like wearing jewelry.

Doing so was a way of displaying social status. But no matter the gifts my father and family gave her, it didn't change a thing.

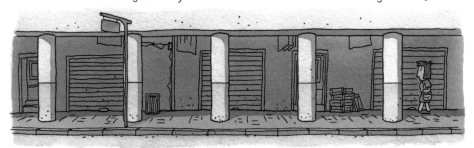

She didn't like making herself up either, even though most Iraqi women wouldn't dream of going out without makeup.

And forget about fur coats in winter.

Napping after lunch at 3:00 p.m. wasn't in her nature either.

She would read instead, or take a walk under the scorching sun, alone in the city with its closed shops.

To get me ready to continue my schooling in France after the move, my mother called on Father Vincent, a Dominican priest and family friend.

He came to the house to help me with my French reading and writing skills.

But we spent more time talking and laughing. He liked to joke around and was always cheerful.

One of the many times my parents organized a party at our place, he asked if he could bring the prince of Albania.

My mother laughed about it on the phone, but it wasn't a joke, and the prince of Albania came to our home.

He was dressed in a normal suit. It was a bit disappointing...

My mother often felt uncomfortable because she wasn't a practicing Christian. One day, she brought it up with Father Vincent.

I hope you don't mind that I don't come to mass.

You've always given to the Little Sisters of the Poor and you feed the beggars who come to your door.

Plus you never say a bad word about anyone.

Your actions are worth far more than those of some of the faithful who come to pray.

And so Father Vincent came twice a week for my French lessons.

But he also came for my mother's desserts.

He would have come seven days a week if she'd asked.

To receive authorization to leave Iraq, my father enrolled in an implant training program at a dental school in Paris.

When the authorization came through, he sold his clinic in Mosul and went to Paris to find an apartment to rent.

My mother didn't want to return to France. She knew my father wasn't resourceful enough to make it on his own.
And as for herself, she knew that she wouldn't be able to depend on her own family, who had completely ignored her since she was a teen.

But she had no choice, and so she found herself selling our furniture, piece by piece, to family, friends, neighbors... It was all the more difficult because some tried to take advantage of the situation.

We're family. Give us a better deal.

But luckily, many offered their help and support. They knew that in her twenty-three years in Iraq, my mother had found everything she'd lacked before.

We moved into a little apartment by the Jourdain metro station. The name reminded my mother of the Jordan River, which flows near Iraq. But that was a small consolation...

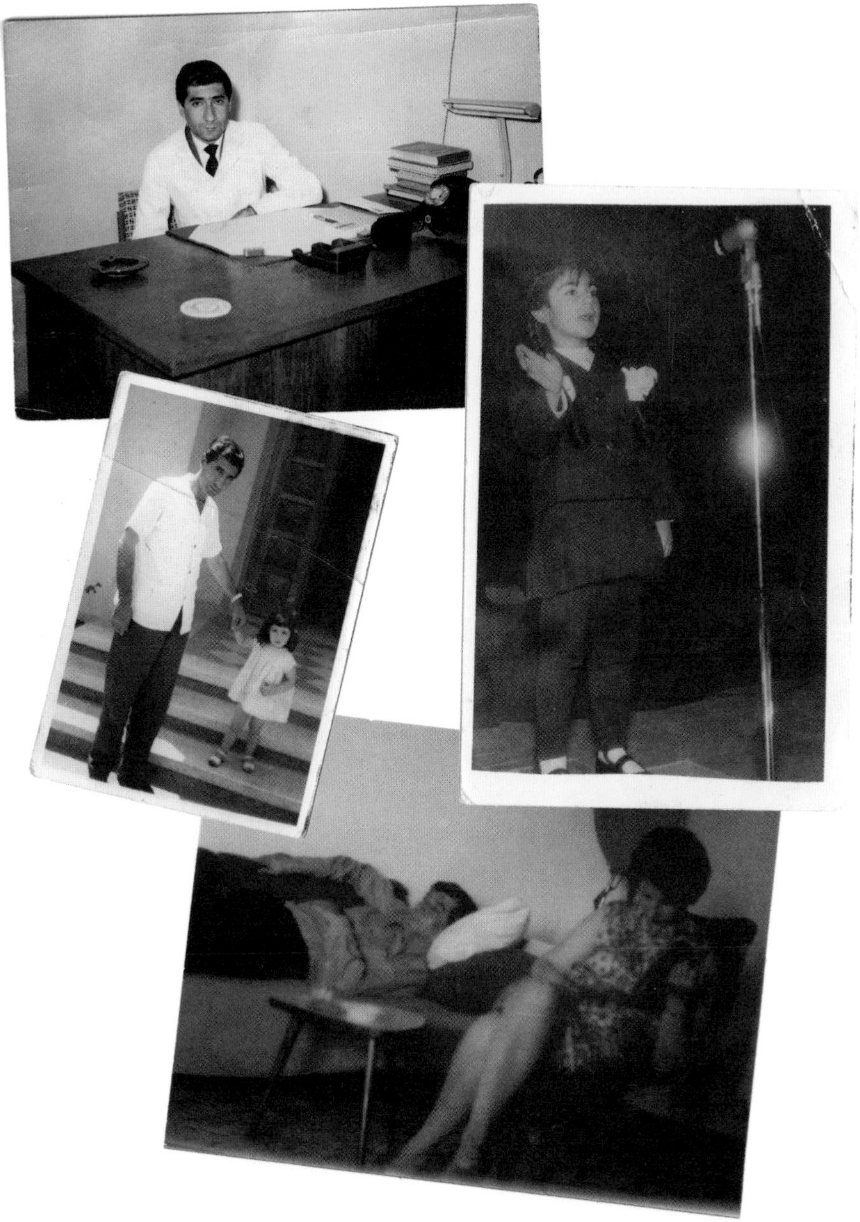

Getting settled in Paris, my mother and I went to the police station in the 20th arrondissement to get our ID cards made.

In my case, there was no problem because I was registered in the family record book, but the agent refused to issue a card for my mother.

You married a foreigner, so you've lost your French citizenship.

But I'm not Iraqi... I've always been French.

Sorry... It's automatic.

No, no, it's not... I was born in France. My parents are French... I even have a French passport.

Ha ha ha

With all the French passports handed out by foreign embassies, I can't just assume it's real.

She insisted, but it was useless. She went back a second time and got no further.

In desperation, she went to the civil office and managed to plead her case to an official. He listened and was appalled.

In front of us, he called the officer at the police station.

But of course this woman is still a French citizen...

You're a disgrace to the nation! I suggest you check the facts before making idiotic statements.

Now you better treat her right and have her card made immediately.

Over at the station, the officer was stonefaced as he handed us the form.

When we received our papers, my name was fine but my mother's was misspelled.

A petty act of revenge by the officer, forcing my mother to go through the process all over again.

After completing his dental implant training program, my father intended to open a clinic. But he was told he couldn't because the degree he had received twenty-five years earlier was a "foreign diploma."

Nonetheless, he worked in a hospital for a few months, which he was allowed to do provided he wasn't paid. And in the meantime, he looked for ways to obtain equivalency.

It turned out that the only way to do so was for him to take the French baccalaureate exam.

Except my father, who was fifty at that point, didn't feel up to it.

That's when he realized the money he had brought from Iraq wasn't enough and he needed to find different work.

My mother looked for a job and became a cashier and bookkeeper for a department store parking lot.

In the meantime, to everyone's surprise, my father decided to sign up as an extra with a casting agency.

He came back to the apartment with nice photo portraits of himself. My mother was perplexed.

He only got hired twice. First there was *The Walls Have Ears*, in which he played a golfer.

The agency had him buy his own golf pants and shoes. Obviously, he didn't make much on that job.

His second performance was as a gangster in *Borsalino and Co.*

But luckily he didn't have to buy a pinstriped Mafia suit or pointy shoes.

When we moved into the Paris apartment, my parents curtained off a part of the living room as their bedroom, and my brother Dominique and I had to share a room.

Since my parents were away at noon, we had to make our own lunch. We discovered instant soups and casseroles, canned ravioli, and processed desserts...

But living with Dominique wasn't always easy. I was thirteen and he was nineteen, and he'd become politically aware and critical of everything.

He listened to jazz and songwriters like Léo Ferré and Georges Brassens... The first record I ever bought was by the French teen idol Sheila. Luckily for him, I didn't like it.

I also bought teen magazines. And I put up posters of the singer Michel Sardou on the wall over my bed, where it faced my brother's, to his despair.

We fought a lot. He thought I was stupid. I thought he was a know-it-all.

The president, Georges Pompidou, died in 1974. To me, he was the "leader of the French Republic that is now my home." And I cried.

My brother mocked me mercilessly.

One time, he recorded songs by Léo Ferré over my cassette of Demis Roussos's greatest hits. I had a fit.

It's crap! They're not even songs!

They're garbage!

And there was the time I played Michel Sardou in an endless loop, and my brother flipped out.

I want to rape women and force them to admire me

Just listen to the lyrics! Listen and think about what he's saying!

I finally moved on to Georges Moustaki.

Before I started eighth grade at the public secondary school, my mother explained to the principal that I spoke excellent French but had never really learned to read or write it.

Understood... I'll let all the teachers know.

My excitement about living in France faded quickly. It all turned into a nightmare, especially in my German class, where the teacher deducted one point for every mistake made in French.

Findakly, zero, again...

Most difficult of all was probably my first essay assignment...Not because it had to be written in French...

But she didn't. I had to explain it to every single teacher, and some didn't believe me.

Take out a sheet of paper and tell me about yourselves.

Still, I was amazed at how the students spoke in class... In Iraq, silence was absolute.

...but because I had to express a personal opinion on a subject, something we were never asked to do in Iraq.

I failed eighth grade, and at the end of ninth grade, my French was still bad enough that I was doing poorly in my other classes as a result.

The guidance counselor recommended that I switch to a vocational secretary training program. I came home in tears and said I didn't want to be a secretary.

It had been bad enough a year earlier, when the reality of everything had sunk in. There were no more discoveries to make up for the everyday hardships.

The shopping, cleaning, cooking, and constant budgeting were a strain, and I missed our life in Mosul.

My parents finally enrolled me in private school in the 2nd arrondissement. Many of the kids had fathers in the military or wealthy families. The atmosphere was pretty racist.

So much so that one day the French teacher, who considered racism natural and logical, put the question to the class.

Who here would claim to not be racist?

You, of course. But that doesn't count.

But how can you say you're racist and still talk to me?

Well, in your case, it's different.

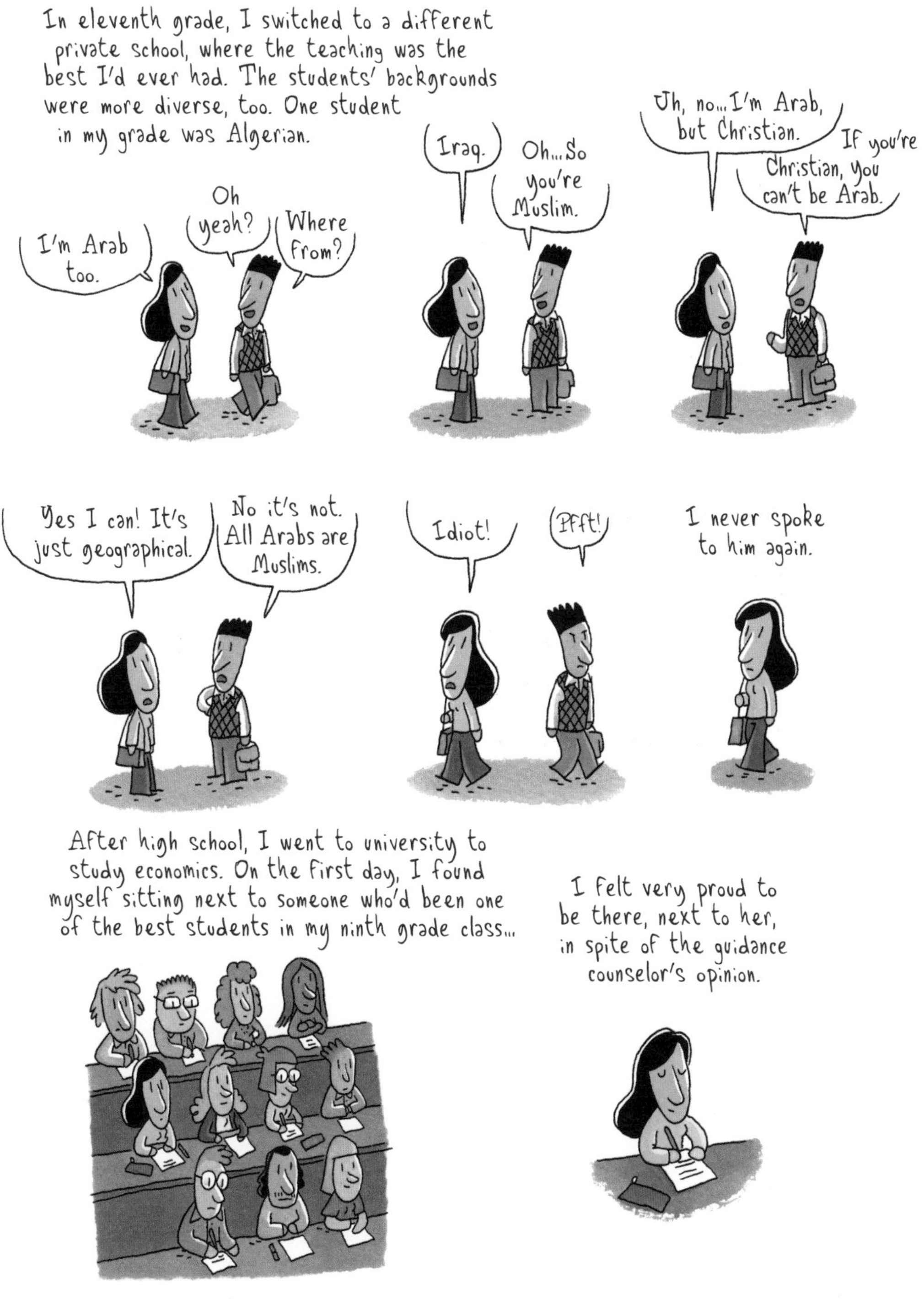
In eleventh grade, I switched to a different private school, where the teaching was the best I'd ever had. The students' backgrounds were more diverse, too. One student in my grade was Algerian.
I'm Arab too.
Oh yeah?
Where from?
Iraq.
Oh...So you're Muslim.
Uh, no...I'm Arab, but Christian.
If you're Christian, you can't be Arab.
Yes I can! It's just geographical.
No it's not. All Arabs are Muslims.
Idiot!
Pfft!
I never spoke to him again.
After high school, I went to university to study economics. On the first day, I found myself sitting next to someone who'd been one of the best students in my ninth grade class...
I felt very proud to be there, next to her, in spite of the guidance counselor's opinion.

In 1977, I returned to Iraq for the first time in four years. I spent the month of July at one of my aunts', in Baghdad.

Not used to the extreme summer heat anymore (up to 50°C), I almost fainted in the street a few times.

Walking through the city and in stores, I was struck by all the portraits of the president and vice president.

They'd been there four years ago too, but now they felt overwhelming.

I mentioned it to my cousin.

It's crazy the way their photos are everywhere.

Shhh...

You can't say that kind of thing in public.

I was starting to become incompatible with Iraq.

Looking for work in France, my father finally went to the Iraqi embassy to see if they could use his services.

He was given a permanent position in a medical clinic. His work mostly involved receiving gravely ill civilians and soldiers wounded during the Kurdish rebellion. He monitored the patients and translated for the French doctors.

In 1978, I returned to Iraq with my mother, this time to Mosul.

My hometown had clearly regressed. Shoulders and knees had to be covered up, although they could still be shown in Baghdad.

And people would comment when I passed by, probably because of my Western clothing, plain as it was.

Look at that foreigner...

It all added up to me not feeling at home anymore.

My aunt received many marriage proposals for me. I politely declined each one. I had never wanted an arranged marriage. And I felt less and less inclined to ever live here again.

One evening, my mother and I went to visit a couple of old friends.

I hope it was just the embassy and that your husband is all right.

?!

Haven't you heard about the Palestinian hostage-taking at the Iraqi embassy in Paris?

We called home and my brother reassured us.

He's fine.

He was in his office. He and the others locked themselves into a closet.

In the end, the Palestinian surrendered to the police. But the Iraqi guards opened fire on him when he came out into the street. One inspector died. The guard who killed him had a diplomatic passport and was able to return to Iraq.

Our car, which had been parked in the street, was punctured by a bullet. And for a while, whenever it rained, I'd catch the water that dripped through in a glass.

In eleventh grade, I had a feminist German teacher. We would take time in class to talk about current events.

I had experienced the huge inequalities between men and women in Iraq, but she made me realize that things in France were far from perfect, and that it wasn't all inevitable.

That's when I started to go to feminist rallies.

Coming from Iraq, I felt like I was committing a huge act of political rebellion.

Protesting was not in my parents' blood, though. They knew what I was up to, but we never spoke about it.

One evening after a demonstration, the TV news reported on the event. I was suddenly terrified that my father might recognize me among the protesters.

The Iran-Iraq war broke out in 1980. My cousin Nabil was a doctor on the front.

Shelling destroyed his medical unit. He was the only survivor, with a broken jaw and shell shards in his body and skull.

No help arrived and so he wandered around for more than a week. In lucid moments, he ate whatever plants and insects he could find.

When he was finally found, he was taken for dead and dropped onto a pile of corpses in the back of a truck.

At the hospital, the people identifying the bodies saw that Nabil was still breathing.

Nabil is alive today and a doctor with Caritas in Baghdad. Physically, he looks twenty years older than his age.

In order to move up in government, another cousin joined the
army for a few months during
the Iran-Iraq war.

Young Iranian soldiers would
attack his position. Many were blown
up by landmines as they crossed
the field in front of him.

The hundreds of others who managed
to get through were mowed down by my
cousin and the other soldiers, who fired
on them with heavy machine guns. It
was the same scenario every day.

The Iranian soldiers all wore a
necklace with a golden plastic key
that their recruiters said would
let them go directly to heaven.

Many Iraqi soldiers wound up
spending some time in psychiatric
hospitals after those massacres.

After his army service, my uncle
became the director general of the
National Alcohol Bureau, notably a
producer of beer and arak.

But under cover of the arak distillery, he imported ingredients that were then transferred to other sites to produce mustard gas and other chemical weapons.

For a number of years, even after the war, my cousin would receive calls in the middle of the night, three to four times a week, ordering him to report immediately to the Ministry of Industry and Armements.

Most times, it was simply to confirm a meeting or for technical questions that could have been settled by phone.

The managers of all the other pharmaceutical and food plants that imported ingredients of military value got the same late-night calls.

The minister, Husayn Kamel al-Majid, who was Saddam Hussein's son-in-law and cousin, eventually fled to Jordan in a Mercedes with his wife and hundreds of thousands of dollars in cash. He wanted to become head of the opposition but they weren't interested.

Saddam Hussein promised to pardon him if he came back with his daughter. And so he returned to Iraq. His divorce was proclaimed the moment they crossed the border and al-Majid was promptly executed.

In 1980, while I was studying economics, I took dance classes. I became friends with the teacher, who was married to a comics artist.

Thanks to him, I learned all about the field. When he saw that I was interested in coloring, he let me have some materials to play around with in my free time.

I'd regularly show him what I was doing, and he eventually offered me some real work for publishers.

After six months, coloring was taking up most of my time and I was starting to make a living from it. I quit university without telling my parents. And then, when my first book came out, I went to see my father. I showed him my name in the credits and told him how much I had earned.

I really love doing this and I'm going to drop out of school.

Oh?

OK

...

All right.

Three years later, I bought a little studio. Being an Iraqi, my father couldn't imagine me living on my own. To keep him from worrying, I said it was just so I could go work there during the day.

One month later, I told him that all the commuting was a bit complicated. And that's how I was able to move out without too much trouble...

In October 1989, one year after the end of the Iran-Iraq war, I returned to Baghdad. Eleven years had gone by since my last trip.

The shock was much greater than the other times.

Of course we had all grown older, but more than anything, my relatives seemed worn out and tired...

A bit like their homes, where cracks went unfixed and loose tiles weren't replaced because of a shortage of building materials.

My female cousins had stopped working. They were married and had children.

We used to have drinks together before dinner, but now they were busy serving their husbands.

After work, my male cousins now changed into a djellaba.

Have a seat... Come...

They all had huge freezers in their homes, which they would fill up whenever stores were restocked between shortages.

There were no bare shoulders to be seen in the city. And skirts had to cover the knees.

My cousins were always examining, touching, and admiring my clothes, as though I was some kind of department store.

I would have happily given my clothes to them, but I was so skinny by comparison.

Portraits of Saddam Hussein hung in every house I visited.

I don't understand why you put up his picture.

We have no choice.

Every family has to.

But be careful around the kids.

At school, somebody comes by every day and asks them what their parents think about Saddam Hussein.

Hymns in praise of Saddam were sung in schools... And propaganda songs played constantly on TV.

You are our sun You are our moon ♫♫♪ Our wounds are healed Even death fears you

I saw my cousin Nabil again, the doctor who had been wounded during the war and left for dead.

The two of us and his brother Emil were about the same age, while all my other cousins were older. I played with them a lot. Nabil was sweet and would go along with anything.

Now, he was seated across from me in the restaurant, with the bottom of his face rebuilt. He was prematurely bald and stooped, almost hunchbacked, and he seemed very fragile.

I couldn't bring myself to look him in the face.

I was told that during the war, when a son died on the front, the family would receive a significant sum of money and a car.

But sometimes the son would come back a few months after his "death."

And occasionally parents would turn their sons away to keep what they'd received.

My cousin Ptisam used to teach art. She had picked up some empty shell casings to make lamps for her living room, and she proudly showed them to me.

My cousin Emil had opened a bakery. His cakes were very similar to American cakes with lots of frosting. Just for a change, I offered to make a French apple tart for everybody.

Another one of my cousins went out to buy apples. I made the tart and then they started cutting it up into equal slices.

I saw that they were dividing up the pieces as fairly as possible and scraping up every last crumb.

Don't worry about it, I'll make another one.

Brigitte, I don't think you realize... With the cost of apples, making another one is out of the question.

It's true...

You can hardly get any fruit in Iraq. My kids don't even know what a banana is.

Everybody confirmed that apples were a rarity and outrageously expensive. Luckily, the tart had turned out all right.

Despite all the shortages, stress, and hardships, my family was starting to see small improvements now that the war was over.

Knowing that I did a bit of drawing, my cousin brought me to the ministry to meet the person...
We were very well received.

I was flattered by the proposal. And I was interested in getting serious about drawing, as well as publishing a book in Iraq. So I agreed to look at the story.

An architect cousin told me that construction was starting up again and that an acquaintance at the Ministry of Culture wanted to make illustrated children's books.

This senior civil servant was thrilled to hear that an Iraqi woman was working in France, and he offered me paid work illustrating a children's book.

But after some serious thought, I realized that if I worked for the Ministry of Culture, I'd be working for Saddam Hussein.

That put a chill on things and I never pursued the idea.

To spend more time with my family,
I extended my stay in Iraq
by two weeks.

Even though I was happy
to be with them, I often had
stomach cramps and nausea.

I saw how much the quality of my
cousins' lives had deteriorated, and
how lucky I was to live in France.

I felt bad for them...
I wanted to save them all but
I knew I couldn't.

The day before I left, my stomach
was in a knot, but in the end I told
them I'd see them again soon.

At least now that the war with Iran
was over, I could go back more often.

Less than a year later, Saddam
Hussein invaded Kuwait, starting
the Gulf War.

I would never see Iraq again.

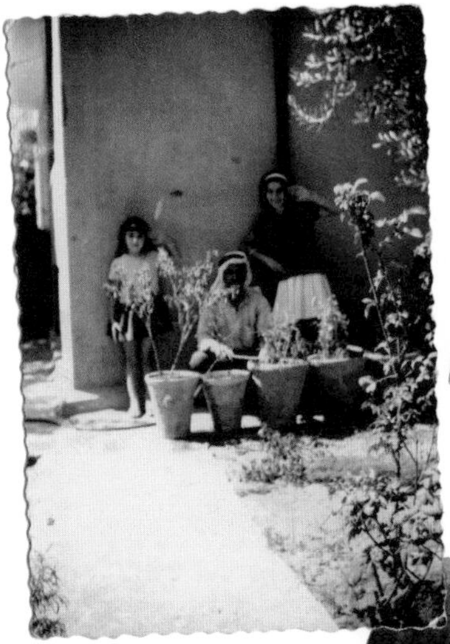

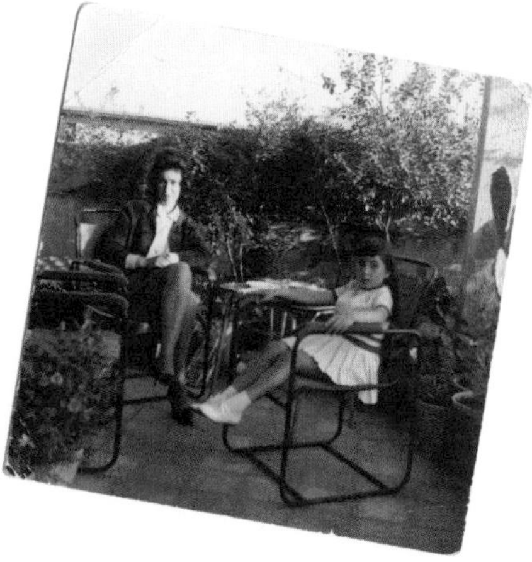

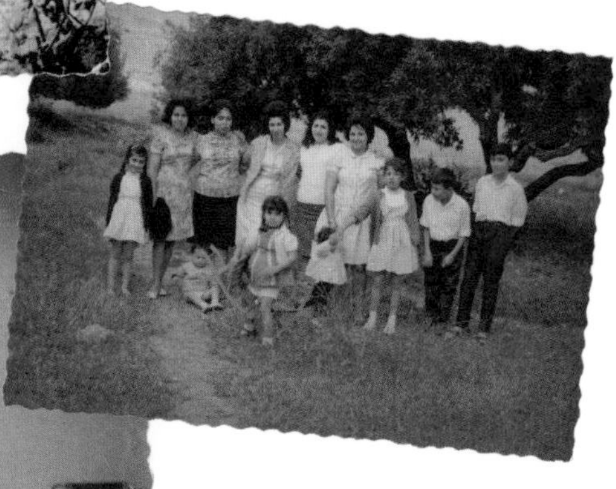

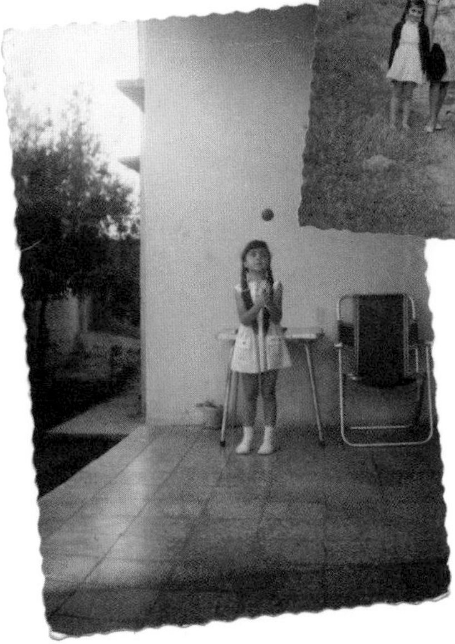

The good memories.

Whenever the shoeshine man passed through the neighborhood, I was the one in charge.

I rounded up all the shoes.

I went to get the money.

I'd sit there and watch him.

His box with its tidy compartments fascinated me.

I loved the smell of the wax.

I wanted to be a shoeshine woman.

My father received a small military pension via the Iraqi embassy, where he had been working since 1975.

In 1980, the Iraqi state decided to stop paying pensions to Iraqis living abroad. Not only that, but retirees abroad were asked to reimburse everything.

The only recourse was to return to Iraq and reapply for a pension. But my father didn't see himself going back.

Since he was still a reservist, he worried that he might not be able to get out of Iraq again and would have to reimburse his pension.

Then, in 1985, all embassy employees were required to join the Baath party. My father didn't want to and so he quit.

He stayed at home after that, sinking into a kind of depression. He regretted having left Iraq and not being able to return for good.

It was all a mistake.

I could have had a wonderful life in Iraq.

My brother and I told him about the changes in Iraq, the shortages and the stress... We told him that, on the contrary, he had given us a better life. That calmed him down for a few months, and then it started all over again.

So when a group of Iraqis he knew decided to travel to Baghdad in 1995, we all encouraged him to go along.

The trip was unsafe. They had to go through Jordan, then take a bus on a desert road and risk being robbed.

Once there, he didn't want to sort out the pension problem, still afraid he'd have to repay the little he'd received twenty years earlier.

He visited his family and saw the situation they were in. After that, he never returned to Iraq and he stopped complaining about having come to France.

In 2007, after Saddam Hussein was ousted, one of my cousins in Baghdad took up the matter with the new government and my father's pension payments were reinstated.

Then, in 2013, even with life certificates authenticated by city hall, the Iraqi state refused to believe that my father was still alive and discontinued his pension.

The good memories.

In winter, the main rooms were heated by a gas stove.

For our bedrooms, my mother made us hot water bottles.

My father often came home late.

When I was already asleep, he would roast chestnuts on the gas stove...

And he'd put them on my nightstand for me to find in the morning.

In 2006, my brother and I went to Amman, Jordan, for the wedding of a cousin's daughter with an Iraqi from New Zealand.

The wedding couldn't be held in Baghdad because it had become too dangerous. A number of churches had been targeted by bomb attacks.

It had been seventeen years since I'd last seen them. And thirty-six years for my brother.

We all cried.

For a long time.

Joy and sorrow marked the wedding, since the bride was leaving for New Zealand right after and her parents didn't know if they would ever see her again.

My family seemed even more ground down this time—by the shortages, the endless power outages, and, above all, the constant and intense worrying about their kids. And they no longer saw a future for themselves.

Bombings were always a threat and the many kidnappings had given way to a racket where thugs would threaten to kidnap people one day and come back for protection money the next.

The police force was in chaos and the Americans were protecting nothing but their own interests.

One day, my cousin Sabah was notified that the school his two sons attended had been bombed.

I went straight over and thank God they weren't hurt.

But the situation in the schoolyard was terrible...there was blood...dead students...

At one point, I saw a boy whose clothes were partly torn.

He was crying...

In front of me, he took off a sock to wipe away his tears.

He told the story in a way that was so tragic and yet so absurd that we couldn't help laughing.

Another cousin who was there had become an alcoholic. He was an optician and his shop was blown up one morning just before he arrived.

A cousin admitted to me that if she and her husband were not living in Iraq, she would have divorced him long ago.

She didn't give any details, but it was the first time I heard talk of divorce in my family.

They finally emigrated a few years later.
But she didn't get a divorce.

One afternoon, three of the husbands left while we were chatting.

Okay... We're off to see the girls.

I wasn't sure I understood what they meant, so I mentioned it to my brother.

What was that earlier about going to see the girls?

It's what you think it is.

So they were off to visit prostitutes, and their wives knew it.

Although one of my cousins seemed annoyed, the women weren't shocked by the announcement.

They considered it normal for the men to get their "relief" elsewhere.

As long as they came home to sleep.

On their way to Baghdad after the wedding, my family narrowly escaped being robbed in the desert.

The taxi ahead of them was pulled over by fake cops and robbed.

Since they were in a caravan, they had each other's phone numbers. The taxi was able to warn the others, who drove on without stopping.

It's 2016. For a long time my cousins hoped things would get better. They stayed until their parents died, and then, to give their children a normal future, almost all of them left, emigrating to the four corners of the earth.

Australia, New Zealand, Canada, the U.S., Sweden, France...

Many have clung to the one thing they could take with them: their Christian faith. And all have become Islamophobic.

I'm not judging them.

I won't try to argue.

I'll continue to love them as they are, as people I care about.

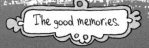

The good memories.

Sandstorms could hit Mosul several times a year.

Everything became orangey yellow.

I would spend hours looking at the sky.

The schools would close and all traffic would come to a stop.

I loved those moments when we all had to stay home together.

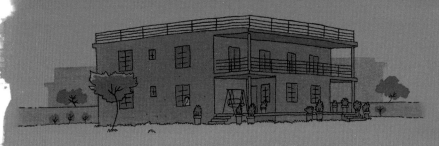

Brigitte Findakly & Lewis Trondheim

4500–2006 BCE	Sumerian civilization in Mesopotamia. Birth of writing and invention of the wheel and beer.
1894–1255 BCE	Babylonian empire. First known code of law.
1255 – 624 BCE	Assyrian empire.
334 BCE	Alexander the Great conquers Babylon.
200 BCE	Writing of the Babylonian Talmud.
226–651	Sasanian empire. Religious tolerance toward Nestorians (future Chaldean Catholics), Jacobites (future Syriac Orthodox Christians), and Jews.
635	The Arab-Muslim conquest begins.
750–1258	Abbasid caliphate. Foundation of Baghdad in 762. Iraq becomes the center of the caliphate.
1258–1534	Mongol invasions.
1534–1917	Ottoman Mesopotamia.
1916	The secret Sykes-Picot Agreement divides the Middle East between France and Britain.
1920–1932	British Mandate.
1924	Election of a Constituent Assembly, February 25. First constitution, June 14.
1927	First oil field found in Kirkuk.
1932–1958	Hashemite Kingdom.
1936	Military coup, the first in the modern Arab world but short-lived.
1941	Nationalist coup led by Ali al-Kaylani drives out the regent's government, April 1. British military intervention ousts al-Kaylani's pro-Nazi regime in late May. Pogrom against Jews erupts in Baghdad.
1958	Coup topples the monarchy. Iraq is declared a republic.
1959–1968	Series of coups and counter-coups by pan-Arab Nasserists, communists, and Baathists (advocates of secular socialist nationalism).
1968	Baath Party takes power in a coup led by General al-Bakr, assisted by Saddam Hussein.
1972	Nationalization of Iraqi petroleum.
1978	Iraq expels the Ayatollah Khomeini to France.
1979	Saddam Hussein takes power.
1980	Iraq attacks Iran, now the Islamic Republic under the leadership of Ayatollah Khomeini. One million dead on each side. Ceasefire in 1988, with original borders restored.
1990	Iraq invades Kuwait. UN sanctions and start of international embargo, deliberately upheld by Saddam Hussein, resulting in the deaths of some 500,000 Iraqis, most of them children.
1991	In January, an international coalition attacks Iraq. In February, Saddam Hussein accepts a ceasefire and withdraws from Kuwait.
1995	UN "oil-for-food" resolution.
2003	In March, the US and Britain attack Iraq. Fighting ends April 15.
2006	Saddam Hussein is tried, sentenced to death, and executed.
2011	American troops withdraw from Iraq.
2014	Daesh captures Mosul and a part of northwestern Iraq.

Brigitte Findakly was born in Mosul, Iraq, in 1959 and lived there until 1973. Findakly has worked as a colorist since 1982, with work for Disney and Spirou. She also colored a number of graphic novels including *The Rabbi's Cat*, *The Spiffy Adventures of McConey*, and *Ralph Azham*.

Lewis Trondheim was born in Fontainebleau, France, in 1964. A cartoonist by profession, his acclaimed works translated into English are *Approximate Continuum Comics*, *Ralph Azham*, *Dungeon* (with Joann Sfar), *The Spiffy Adventures of McConey* and *A.L.I.E.E.E.N.* Trondheim is also the cofounder of the legendary comic house L'Association, cofounder of L'OuBaPo, and director of the Shampooing graphic novel imprint.

Findakly and Trondheim have two children and live in the south of France.